COUNTERPOINT

THE MACMILLAN COMPANY
NEW YORK · CHICAGO
DALLAS · ATLANTA · SAN FRANCISCO
LONDON · MANILA

IN CANADA
BRETT-MACMILLAN LTD.
GALT, ONTARIO

COUNTERPOINT

An Introduction to Polyphonic Composition

HUGO KAUDER

New York
The Macmillan Company
1960

First Printing

The Macmillan Company, New York
Brett-Macmillan Ltd., Galt, Ontario

Printed in the United States of America

Library of Congress catalog card number: 60–6643

The forms of music are the forms of eternal things.

—F. W. J. Schelling

The invisible harmony is stronger than the visible.

—Heraclitus

Preface

The teachings of this book are based on a new concept of tonality, whose theoretical foundations are laid down in the introductory chapter. Counterpoint itself is merely a practical discipline, neither a theoretical nor a historical one. Yet it has been, and still is, taught as the latter, throughout more than two centuries. In a period when chordal harmony became more and more predominant, an earlier polyphonic art was the only remaining source for the teaching and practice of counterpoint. Since that time the ghost of "strict counterpoint" has been haunting the teaching of musical composition, imposing on teachers and students the limitations—often only imaginary—of the art of a remote past. Thus counterpoint has been alienated more and more from the present musical life and has become a kind of musical scholarship, on the one hand taught as such, on the other discredited.

The teachings of this book are strict none the less. Their strictness, however, is conditioned first of all by the purity and severity of intellectual and artistic principles, secondly by the fundamentals of craftsmanship, equally valid for the master and the student, and finally by the old pedagogical principle of starting within narrow limits and widening them gradually by proceeding from the simple to the complicated.

Such strictness requires that this book be based and centered on tonality, notwithstanding the fact that in today's musical life tonality is no more recognized as a principle of general validity. It is true that, owing to a long and consistent development, traditional tonality has lost its moving and shaping force, thus having become indifferent. It has been replaced by the artificial constructions of the "twelve-tone system," today widely regarded as the last word of music history. Yet it has to be said, with due reverence for Arnold Schoenberg's great personality, that it can not be more than a mere expedient in a period of crisis and transition, and that even the most ingenious artifice sooner or later will be superseded by an art grown out of the moving and shaping forces of music itself. As these forces are inherent in the very substance of music, they will be rejuvenated, whenever time makes it necessary, out of the primordial source of music: the order of the universe and the accordance of human nature with this order.

There is, however, no need of a thoroughly new method of counterpoint teaching. Counterpoint is merely the technique of polyphonic composition; its basic elements can be taught and its highest accomplishments reached on the grounds of any tonal system and applied to any temporal or individual style. Thus the traditional method of counterpoint teaching has been adapted here to the new principles of tonality.

The author wishes to give thanks to all those who assisted him in giving this book its final shape:

to Mr. Clifford Richter, who prepared the manuscript for the printer and especially spent the greatest care on the arrangement of the musical examples;

to Mr. Carl A. Rosenthal, the autographer of the musical examples, who far beyond his expert calligraphical work was a careful and interested collaborator with the author;

to Professor Siegmund Levarie for his assistance in reading the proofs and for many valuable suggestions;

to his son Otto Kauder for help and advice during the whole
work and for typing the finished manuscript; and

to all the staff members of the publishing house, who took part
in the production of the book, for their most careful work and,
in many cases, their friendly and untiring cooperation with the
author.

New York,
on Bach's 275th birthday

Contents

Theoretical Foundations

Basic Tonal Relations—The Scale

Counterpoint is the technique of polyphonic composition, the art of uniting two or more voices, i.e. *melodies*, to *one* polyphonic harmony. Thus counterpoint is not a theoretical discipline but an eminently practical one. Its teaching and practice, however, must be based on a theory built on fundamental facts and establishing a tonal system of general validity, this all the more in the present age, in which the traditional tonal system has been shaken, and the language of music is undergoing a process of change. Therefore it is of no avail to teach the elements of composition any longer according to any temporal style, be it a "modern" one or the more or less imaginary style of an earlier epoch. Only on principles of general and lasting validity can a theory and technique be developed which can be applied to any musical idiom and any individual or temporal style.

Such principles can be derived from the basic tonal relations determined by the physical fact that the pitch of any tone is directly proportional to the frequency of the tone-producing vibra-

1

tions and inversely proportional to the length of the tone-producing body. Thus the elementary tonal relations can be expressed by equally elementary numerical relations.

As all these tonal relations can be constructed in a twofold way, upward and downward, they are expressed by two opposite series of numbers: one is the sequence of the prime numbers 1, 2, 3, 5, and their multiples, representing the rising order of basic tonal relations. The other, in descending order, is the reciprocal series of fractions with the numerator 1.

1 being the length and vibration-frequency of an open string, one-half of this string produces the upper octave, by twice as many vibrations. One-third of the string produces the upper 12th, by three times as many vibrations, and so on. According to the same physical law, the same intervals are produced in descending order by multiplying the string length.

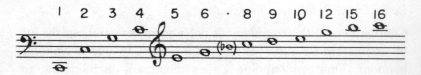

These two rows of tones, representing the basic intervals, are ranked in order according to their degree of blending together, i.e. *consonance* (consonare: to sound together). The octave is the most perfect consonance, its two tones almost completely blending into one when sounded together. The two tones of each of the following intervals are more discernible: the fifth and the fourth are still recognized as "perfect" consonances; the major and minor third and also the major and minor sixth are "imperfect" consonances, their simultaneous sound being perceived as a harmonious unit. The two tones of the major second, and even more those of the minor second, are sharply discernible when sounded at the same time; they even have a certain tendency to move apart, which we call *dissonance* (dissonare: to sound asunder).

The intervals of the two series of partial tones, when brought into the space of one octave, form a conjunct sequence of tones called the *scale*.

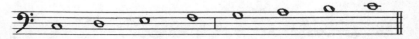

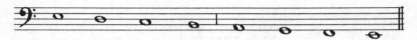

The scale up from C, derived from the ascending sequence of partial tones, therefore reveals its true nature most evidently in the ascending direction; this becomes evident especially in the closing half step from the leading tone to the tonic. Hence we call it the *ascending* or *rising* scale. Correspondingly the scale down from E, derived from the descending sequence of partial tones, reveals its nature in the descending direction and hence is called the *descending* or *falling* scale.

Each scale contains three forms of step-progression: the major whole step 9:8, the minor whole step 10:9, the half step 16:15. The difference between the major and the minor whole step, expressed by the ratio 81:80 and known as the *syntonic comma*, is imperceptible to the human ear and therefore disregarded by musical practice. Thus for our ear the scale appears to consist of two equal tetrachords.

The two opposite series of partial tones and the two scales derived from them are the sounding realization of the *universal law of polarity*. Polarity, the primordial moving force of the uni-

verse and the origin of life on earth, also has generated the basic
elements of music.

A third tetrachord, up or down from d, with the half step in the
middle, is contained in both rows of tones. Hence a scale can be
formed by two tetrachords of this structure. Neither the rising nor
the falling sense is prevalent in this scale, therefore it has to be considered *ambivalent* or *neutral*. While the falling scale is the inversion (or, notated in the bass clef, the mirror image) of the rising
scale, the neutral scale remains the same when inverted.

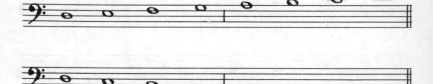

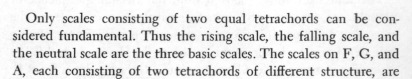

Only scales consisting of two equal tetrachords can be considered fundamental. Thus the rising scale, the falling scale, and
the neutral scale are the three basic scales. The scales on F, G, and
A, each consisting of two tetrachords of different structure, are
of secondary importance.

Deriving the basic intervals and scales from *one* tone by divid-
ing or multiplying the tone-producing string-length means infi-
nitely more than a mere arithmetical procedure, for sound is
movement, just as light and life are movement. Owing to these
arithmetical relations, the scale is a *measured* movement. Its fundamental tone is the generator of this movement and its center of
gravitation. This gravitation—we call it *tonality*—is the moving
force and produces the inner life of music, thus making music a
likeness of the order and movement of the universe. According to
its function as a center of gravity, the fundamental tone has to be
placed in the center in order to give to the scale its most perfect
shape:

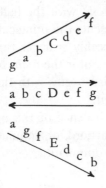

This "closed scale" has to be unfolded in order to make it move, starting and ending with the tonic. In its unfolded form, or *resolution*, the closed scale appears as a prototype of melody, its tones performing a circular movement around the tonic, in perfect balance between rising and falling.

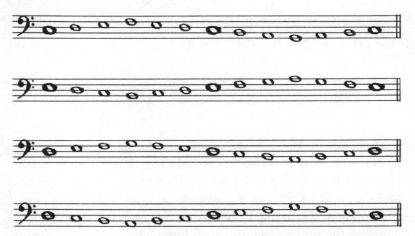

The attractive force toward the central tone reaches the maximum in the two outermost tones of the closed scale, the upper and lower fourth from the tonic. These are the opposite poles and turning points of the scale, the *dominants*.

The tetrachord that closes with the half step, in the rising and in the falling scale, represents the principal sense of the scale, and its moving force is noticeably stronger than that of the opposite tetrachord. We therefore call it the *main tetrachord*, the other the *counter-tetrachord*; the first begins with the *dominant*, the second with the *counterdominant*.

According to the ambivalence of the neutral scale there is no prevailing direction, tetrachord, or dominant; one can only speak of an upper and a lower dominant.

$$
\begin{array}{cccccc}
 & & & & +C & \\
 & & +T & d & e & f \\
 & & C & & & \\
+D & a & b & & & \\
g & & & & & \\
{}^\circ D+ & & {}^\circ T & & {}^\circ D- & \\
a & b & c & D & e \quad f \quad g & \\
-D & & & & & \\
a & g & f\,{}^{-}T & & & \\
 & & E & d & -C & \\
 & & & c & b & \\
\end{array}
$$

T Tonic	+ Ascending direction
D Dominant	− Descending direction
C Counterdominant	° Ambivalence

The scales on F, G, A, and B are *mixed scales,* each consisting of two dissimilar tetrachords. Accordingly, their tonality is ambiguous; the tone on which they begin and end is not the generator-tone of the scale, but a *pseudo-tonic,* functioning as a tonic without, however, having its full force. Therefore it is of no avail to represent the mixed scales in closed form. The tonality of each of these scales has to be ascertained by investigating its relationship to the fundamental scales.

The scale on G consists of the rising tetrachord g a b C and the neutral tetrachord D e f g. It can be coördinated with the rising scale, with the real tonic C and the pseudo-tonic G. It can be coördinated also with the neutral scale, having D as the real tonic.

The scale on A is the inversion of that on G and correspondingly related to the falling and neutral scales. It can be coördinated with either of them. In both cases the actual tonality is determined by the musical context.

In the scale of F, and its inversion, that on B, one of the two tetrachords runs through an augmented fourth; therefore only the second tetrachord determines the tonality. Thus the scale on F can be coördinated only with the rising scale, the scale on B only with the falling scale.

Elimination of the two tones which proceed by half steps changes the scale of seven tones to a *five-tone* or *pentatonic* scale. The *rising five-tone scale* is g a C d f; the same five tones with D as tonic result from applying the same procedure to the neutral scale in rising direction. The *falling five-tone scale* is a g E d b; these five tones, with D as tonic, are obtained from the neutral scale in falling direction.

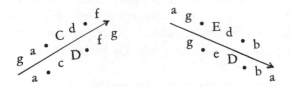

The resolutions of the closed five-tone scales appear below:

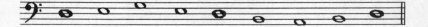

According to the ambivalence of the neutral scale, one can regard the lower tetrachord as rising, the other as falling. The five-tone scale constructed accordingly is symmetrical and the most harmonious of the pentatonic scales.

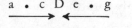

The same five tones constitute two more scales: the rising scale C d e g a c, and its inversion, the falling scale E d c a g e. In both of these the counterdominant is lacking; in return the tonic yields a complete triad according to the sense of the scale. Since primordial ages the first of these scales has been the fundamental scale of Chinese music. It also prevails in Scottish, Irish, and Welsh folk music as a relic of the old Celtic world. In old America all three five-tone scales were represented (see the two American folk tunes in the appendix). There is also a considerable influx of pentatonic elements into Gregorian chant.

The utmost extension of tonality can be achieved by combining the two opposite basic scales on one tone:

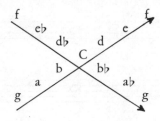

The two opposite scales are hereby united to one hermaphroditic *double scale* of eleven tones, a *diatonic* scale in the original sense of the Greek *dia tonos*, i.e. moving *through the tones*, none of them being omitted, all of them equally essential and centered on the tonic.

In the resolution of the double scale, the tones of the ascending scale occur only in ascending direction, those of the descending scale only in descending direction:

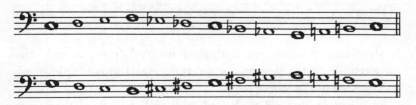

Those who might worry about the missing twelfth tone may be comforted. This tone, although exceeding the space of the closed scale, can be introduced as an auxiliary tone, the upper leading tone of the counterdominant or the lower leading tone of the dominant:

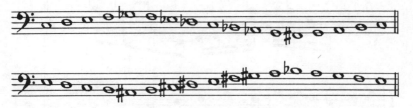

Thus the range of tonality includes thirteen tones, since the two auxiliary tones cannot be interchanged enharmonically, being of opposite sense, one falling, the other rising.

The melodic minor scale is a mixed scale and can be regarded as an incomplete double scale: the falling scale combined with one rising tetrachord.

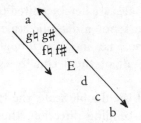

It should be remembered that E is the real tonic, A only the pseudo-tonic of the A minor scale, the natural minor scale being coördinated to the falling scale.

Bach frequently used the raised sixth and seventh of the minor scale also in descending direction, sometimes with regard to the harmony, the major chord of the dominant (example a), sometimes even regardless of it (example b).

J. S. Bach: Well-Tempered Clavier, V. 1

(a)

J. S. Bach: Italian Concerto

(b)

The opposite scale—the rising scale combined with one falling tetrachord—came into use more than one century later and became a principal feature of Romanticism.

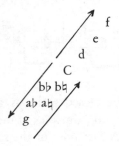

J. Brahms: Symphony No. 4

Melody

The resolution of the closed scale, as a prototype of melody, represents the fundamental principles of melody. The first of them is tonality, which relates the tones of the scale to one central tone in an arithmetically determined order of rank and makes them move around this central tone, thus making the scale a likeness of the order and movement of a solar system. The second principle, which may be called the physical law of melody, is the balance between rising and falling. This balance, however, should not be obtained too easily by too obvious and symmetrical alternation between ascending and descending movement, thus:

This example lies as far as possible away from being a good melody. The inner balance of a good melody becomes apparent in a *step-progression* resulting from the interplay of rising and falling movement, of leaps and steps. Thus the physical law of balance is joined by the principle of organic growth, which is progress. Both are subordinated to the intellectual principle of the scale and its moving and shaping force, tonality.

The interplay of these three principles is shown in the following examples. Among the infinite possibilities of this interplay a few types of melodic movement can be distinguished:

1) stepwise movement counterbalanced by stepwise movement in the opposite direction—

2) leaps counterbalanced by stepwise movement or vice versa—

3) leaps counterbalanced by leaps in opposite direction—

All these examples and as many more as possible should be studied carefully, not by a dissecting analysis but by experiencing melody as *movement*, i.e. a succession of disturbances and restorations of balance.

The student now should proceed to invent melodies of his own. These melodies should be limited to moving in notes of equal value, this for two reasons: first, in order to be concerned with purely melodic considerations without being diverted by considerations of rhythm; second, in order to use the melodies for counterpoint exercises. The melodies should move in whole or half notes, each note representing two beats, and their tonality should be confined to the three basic scales. As a special study, some of them should be kept within the range of the closed scale.

A few rules are given here, much more for guiding the student than for imposing limitations on him:

1) Avoid immediate repetition of a tone; repetition should occur only at a reasonable distance and on a different metric position. The highest and lowest tones of the melody should not be repeated at all. In the following example the tones d and e appear for the first time on the light beat, the second time on the strong beat; once more d appears on the light beat, while f comes first on the strong beat and later on the light beat.

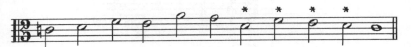

2) Avoid augmented intervals; both tones of an augmented interval function as leading tones, and their progression according to this function increases the tension instead of restoring the balance.

3) Avoid broken triads, since there is little or no melodic progress between tones belonging to one and the same harmonic unit.

4) Abstention from the use of bar lines, as is exemplified throughout this book, will considerably enhance the student's feeling for melodic and rhythmic continuity and coherence. If, in the more complex examples, it becomes necessary or desirable to mark the metric accents, this can be done best by drawing small vertical dashes above the notes. These will serve as bar lines without cutting through the musical context. (See the examples on pages 47 ff.)

Harmony

Chordal harmony emerges from the same principle as the basic relations of melodic succession, both being sounding realizations of fundamental arithmetical ratios.

The tones corresponding to the cardinal numbers 4, 5, 6, as well as the respective reciprocals, produce, when sounded together, a consonant harmony, the triad.

Consequently there are two triads, one the inversion of the other, thus representing the principle of polarity in the vertical dimension. The one—consisting of prime, major third, and fifth in rising direction—is produced by nature as the 3rd, 4th, and 5th overtones of a sounding body. It is generally known as the major chord. In a system that derives its terminology consistently from the principle of polarity, this triad has to be called, according to its origin, the *over-chord*. The other—consisting of prime, major third, and fifth in falling direction—cannot be produced by nature, because a vibrating string can divide but never multiply itself automatically. Known as the minor chord, it must consistently be called the *under-chord*.

The theory and practice of chordal harmony—regarding and treating the chord as a unit—thus seem to contradict the principle and the practice of counterpoint, which deal with individual melodic voices. From a higher viewpoint, however, this contradiction disappears; chords and chord progressions represent the idea of harmony only in its utmost materialization. In its wider and deeper sense, harmony is an intrinsic moving and shaping force that acts in two directions, producing melody as the horizontal, chordal harmony as the vertical dimension of music, uniting both to the intellectual space of polyphony.

The scale, being the structural principle of tone succession, also generates the structural principle of chord progression, the *cadence*. The cadence results from coördinating with the scale those triads which are formed from its tones according to the sense of the scale. Such triads can be formed only on the three principal tones of the scale, namely, the tonic, the dominant, and the counterdominant. Thus the three principal tones of the rising scale generate over-chords, those of the falling scale under-chords.

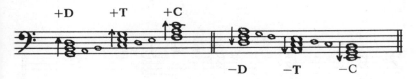

There is an inescapable contradiction: In a sequence of under-chords, polarity cannot be carried through consistently insofar as the lowest tone, the under-fifth, has to function as the fundamental bass, the root of the harmony. Chordal harmony, as it represents the material side of harmony, is not only subject to the universal law of polarity, but is bound also to the terrestrial forces of gravity and of organic life, both irreversible, one tending toward the earth, the other growing up from the earth toward the light. Only the art of counterpoint overcomes this contradiction and dissolves the material chord-harmony into an "invisible harmony" that constitutes a texture of melodies; it overcomes gravity by making bass and top voice interchangeable, thus elevating music from the terrestrial to an intellectual space.

The tension toward the tonic, inherent in the dominant and the counterdominant, also belongs to their chords; the dominant chord has the stronger tension toward the tonic triad, containing, as its third, the leading tone of the scale. This tension toward the tonic acts as moving force, as gravitation, hence the name cadence (fall).

Joining together the two cadences C-T and D-T yields the *complete cadence* T-C-T-D-T, which moves in accordance with the unfolded closed scale, both performing a circuit around the tonic.

The tonic chord in the middle of the above cadence can be omitted, since here the tonic is only transitory.

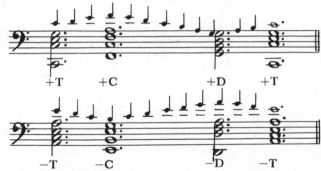

According to the ambiguity and bipolarity of the neutral scale, almost everything in its chord system functions in a contradictory sense; the tonic yields an under-chord in rising direction, an over-chord in falling direction, the upper dominant under-chords and the lower dominant over-chords in both directions.

Owing to the lack of a leading tone, the neutral cadence lacks the closing force of the rising or falling cadence, but this, too, is in full accordance with the character of this scale.

The double scale allows the widest display of both principles, that of polarity and that of tonality, as each of the three principal tones appears in the rising as well as in the falling sense. Therefore two opposite chords are coördinated with each of them.

The complete cadence is shown below:

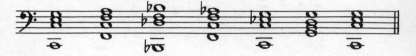

2

The Practice of Counterpoint

TWO-PART SETTING

The Five Species

First Species: Note Against Note

The elementary exercises of counterpoint are based on melodies moving in notes of equal value. The first assignment consists in setting against such a melody a second voice in the same note values, above as well as below, i.e. one note against each note of the given melody. The Latin name of this kind of two-part setting, *punctus contra punctum*, gave to this practice the name *counterpoint*, which name since has been applied to any specific melodic voice set against a given melody, as well as to the art of polyphony in general.

According to the definition of counterpoint, any contrapuntal voice has to be an *independent melody*, although being governed by the tonality and fitted to the meter of the given melody. In relation to each other, two voices can move in four possible ways: *parallel motion*, both voices proceeding in the same direction and in equal intervals; *similar motion*, both voices moving in the same direction, but in different intervals; *contrary motion*, two voices moving in opposite directions; *oblique motion,* one voice moving, the other voice remaining on one tone.

For the sake of the independence of voices, parallel motion in octaves and fifths is strictly forbidden, since two voices proceeding in consecutive perfect consonances are no longer two discernible parts, but the same melody doubled.

Also with regard to the independence of voices, even the use of parallel thirds and sixths should be limited to no more than three, at most four of them.

The prohibition of "antiparallels," i.e. consecutive octaves and fifths reached by contrary motion, is not justified:

There is no real parallelism, since the two parts proceed by different intervals. Owing to the contrary motion the voices are easily discernible, in spite of the consecutive perfect consonances.

The two voices of a contrapuntal setting have to constitute a clearly determined harmony; the harmony is determined by the scale on which the given melody is based. In principle, the harmony can be determined by a dissonance just as well as by a consonance. In these elementary exercises, however, the harmony has to be limited to consonant intervals: octave, fifth, third, sixth. The fourth, although acoustically a perfect consonance, is harmonically ambiguous and therefore its use is bound to special conditions as shown in the following examples:

1) The fourth is a consonance, g being clearly the root of the harmony.

2) The fourth is ambiguous, d could be the root of the harmony, but just as well a passing note between c and e.

3) The fourth is clearly a dissonance, an appoggiatura before the third.

4) The fourth belongs to the previous harmony.

In any case, at least one of the two voices moving to and from the fourth should proceed stepwise.

The counterpoint above the given melody can start with the octave, fifth, or third. The unison should be used only when the voices proceed to the next note by contrary motion.

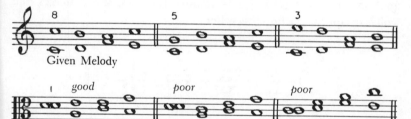

In the lower voice, the counterpoint should start with the octave or unison only (contrary motion in the latter case).

At the end, the octave or unison should always be reached by step-progression in both voices.

However, the lower voice may assume the function and specific character of a *bass*; accordingly, it may finish with a bass cadence.

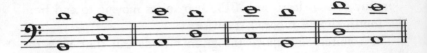

Except on the first and the last notes, the unison should not appear in a two-part setting note against note, because it makes one voice disappear within the other.

The octave sounds best when approached by contrary motion. When it is approached by similar motion, one of the two voices should proceed stepwise. Moreover the octave should consist of the doubled root of the harmony; otherwise its sound will be vague and empty, as in the third of the following examples.

In addition to melody and harmony, the spatial relation of the two parts has to be considered carefully. The distance between the two parts should not exceed the interval of a tenth.

Simultaneous leaps in the same direction, especially when exceeding the third, easily produce spatial disproportion as well as melodic and harmonic disjunction; but instead of anxiously avoiding them, the student should learn to use them with discrimination.

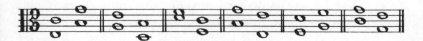

There is no objection against crossing the parts frequently necessitated by melodic considerations. In note-against-note two-part settings, however, the discernibility of the two voices should be considered carefully.

The prohibition of "hidden" or "covered" fifths, i.e. fifths reached by similar motion, is a mere schoolmaster's rule, that has been consistently disregarded by the masters of all times. Therefore it should be banished from the teaching of harmony and counterpoint.

Notwithstanding the obligation of setting consonant harmonies note against note, the main task is to produce *melodies*. Therefore the student, from the very beginning and in spite of all initial difficulties, ought to strive for melodic coherence. While he is concerned with one note, his thought already should be directed toward the next few notes.

Here are a few general directions for the student's work:

1) Everything you are writing down should be imagined as living and sounding music, not just notes set on paper by way of abstract calculation or construction.

2) Do all work *only* by writing, without the help of an instrument (except in cases of special difficulties).

3) After having finished an exercise, sing through each individual voice, then play all together on the piano.

4) Never be discouraged by difficulties; on the contrary, search for them and learn to enjoy the struggle with them. Be strict toward yourself in any regard, in order to acquire the sensitivity and responsibility that make the true artist.

5) Do not be afraid of mistakes, nor be discouraged or ashamed of having made some; the discussion and correction of your mistakes will provide you with indispensable experience.

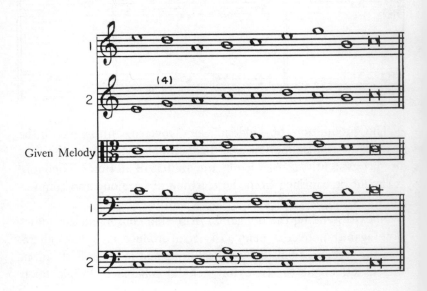

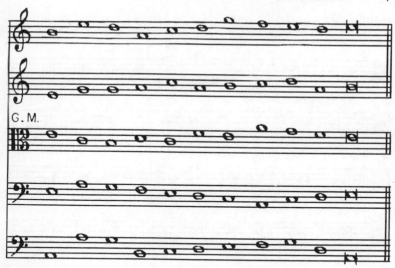

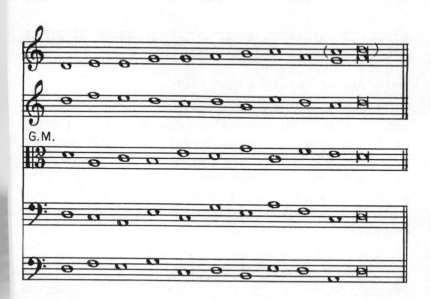

Melodies for Exercises

Second Species: Two Notes Against One

This exercise consists of setting two notes of equal value against each note of the given melody. Here for the first time dissonances may be introduced, but only on the light beat, so-called passing notes proceeding by step from one consonance to another. The strong beat must be a consonance, and the unison should be avoided on strong beats except for the first and last notes. Leaps may occur only between consonances, as shown in the following examples.

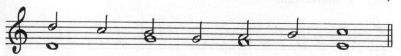

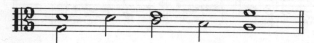

Starting the counterpoint on the second beat enhances the independence of the parts.

The effect of parallel octaves or fifths cannot be eliminated by passing notes between them; only contrary motion between them can make them admissible.

a) is absolutely intolerable; in b) in spite of the intervening contrary motion, the accent on the octaves and fifths is stressed by the sequence; c) is tolerable. Both b) and c) become completely unobjectionable when a third voice is added.

G. M.

G. M.

Three Notes Against One

A setting of three notes against each note of the given melody permits the use of three kinds of dissonances: the passing note on the second beat, the passing note on the third beat, and the neighboring note (also "returning" or "auxiliary" note), i.e. the upper or lower second which returns to the preceding tone. As in the second species, any dissonance must enter and proceed by step, being preceded and followed by a consonance.

Third Species: Four Notes Against One

The third species offers the following possibilities for using dissonances:

a) the passing note on the second and fourth quarters,

b) the passing note on the third quarter,

c) the upper or lower neighboring note on the second or fourth quarter.

Each of these must be preceded and followed by a consonance. (See the following examples.)

There is one more kind of dissonance, the *nota cambiata* (or simply *cambiata*), i.e. *exchanged note*, as here the third and fourth notes of a step-progression are exchanged. Thus the step-progression is interrupted by a leap of a third and restored by the following step in the opposite direction.

Here, *accented octaves* are admissible, being sufficiently counteracted by the intervening contrary motion; not so in the following two examples, since there is only one quarter in between. The last two examples are unobjectionable because the first of the two octaves is not accented.

Cadences:

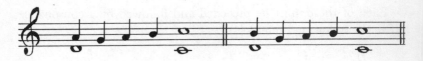

The rules and directions for the third species also apply to the two-part setting of six notes against one. Therefore it will suffice to give the following examples.

Fourth Species: Syncopes

In this species, the counterpoint moves in *syncopes*, i.e. notes of the same value as those of the given melody, but starting one beat later. Each note of the counterpoint enters on the light beat, in consonance with the given melody. On the next strong beat, this same note enters a new harmonic relationship which may be a consonance or a dissonance. If a consonance results, the counterpoint may move by step or by leap to another consonance.

When the counter-note becomes a dissonance, i.e. a suspension, it has to be *resolved* by moving one step downward, into a consonance on the next light beat. If the counterpoint is above the given melody, a second must move to a unison, a fourth to a third, a seventh to a sixth, a ninth to an octave. If the counterpoint is below the given melody, a second goes to a third, a fourth to a fifth, a seventh to an octave, a ninth to a tenth.

The suspension of the lower seventh, however, should not be used except for compelling melodic reasons (as in the above example, the descending step-progression), since a dissonance whose resolution is anticipated in the upper voice, has lost most of its moving force.

The suspension of an upper ninth should never be preceded by an octave, as the resulting *afterbeating octaves* have to be regarded as parallels. Similarly, the suspension of the lower fourth must not be preceded by a fifth.

Some dissonances also may be resolved upward: an upper second to a third, an upper ninth to a tenth, an upper seventh to an octave, and a lower seventh to the sixth, the last especially when moving a half step.

Most of these progressions should be used only where there are compelling reasons of voice leading, however, preferably in settings of more than two parts.

Syncopation ends in the measure before the last, the last note entering simultaneously with the last note of the given melody. The best closing cadences are those made with the suspension of the seventh above, or the second below the given melody.

Syncopation may be interrupted for the sake of better voice leading or harmony (as in the upper voice of the first and second of the following examples). In this case the counterpoint moves as in the second species.

Syncopation produces a simple but effective counterrhythm to the given melody, enriching and intensifying the harmony by creating a dissonance on the strong beat. Therefore it belongs among the principal features of contrapuntal technique and style.

Fifth Species: Notes of Various Values
(Mixed *or* florid *counterpoint*)

Here the counterpoint makes free use of various rhythmic values: halves, dotted halves, quarters, and eighths. Of course, these varying elements have to be united in a consistent and well-proportioned way, and special attention has to be given to smooth and fluent changes between longer and shorter rhythmic values. Changes of rhythm should take place on a light beat.

The first of these two examples is stiff and awkward, the second balanced and fluid.

Also in this exercise syncopation should be used amply. Interrupting the resolution of a suspension by interpolating shorter notes adds rhythmic and melodic variety. The quarter note or the first of two eighths that interrupt the resolution must be consonances. The anticipated resolution, at x, a typical feature of the Palestrina style, should be followed by another suspension.

In all these examples longer notes are tied over to shorter ones. The opposite, i.e. a shorter note tied over to a longer one, is rhythmically awkward and should be avoided.

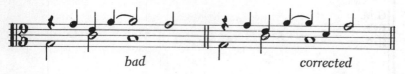

bad   *corrected*

Mixed Note-Values in Both Parts—Vocal Two-Part Settings

The possibility of rhythmic variety in both voices should never lead to overloading them with too many notes (the main danger for the beginner!). The two parts should complement each other rhythmically in such a manner that whenever one of them moves in shorter notes, the other stands on longer ones, as in the following examples.

Melodies for Exercises

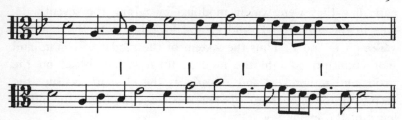

Contrapuntal writing of this kind is a first step beyond mere technical exercise toward composition for two voices. Therefore, this assignment also includes vocal settings on plain chants. Here special care is needed to provide for clear articulation and correct accentuation of the text. To this end the following rules should be observed:

1) No shorter value than one beat should be set to one syllable.

2) A note of half-beat duration should occur only after a dotted note, a syncope, or a sequence of several notes on one syllable, and should be followed by a longer note or a melisma (several notes on one syllable). The last syllable of a sentence should fall on the last note of the melody.

Here a few explanatory remarks on the tonality of the plain chant are needed:

The so-called Gregorian modes (Church modes) are represented by the four "authentic" scales on D, E, F, G; with each of them a "plagal" scale is coördinated, which starts and ends a fourth lower (on A, B, C, D), but has the tonic (called *finalis*, i.e. the ending tone), in common with the authentic mode. Thus the plagal modes differ from the authentic only in their melodic range, not in tonality, and therefore that distinction can be disregarded.

A polyphonic harmony according to the true nature of the modes has never existed. The modes originated in an epoch of purely monophonic music, and even in the earliest practice of

part song they were widely modified by raising the seventh degree in the scales on D and G and lowering B to B-flat in the
scales on D and F. Thus the system of the modes was more and
more transformed into the modern tonal system based on the
major and minor key, and as early as the eleventh century the
theory of the hexachord ut-re-mi-fa-sol-la established the preva-
lence of the major key.

Our concept of tonality makes it possible to develop a thoroughly
consistent polyphony according to the original tonality of the
modes. Thus the first mode, on D, should be identified with our
neutral scale; the second, on E, with the falling scale. The 3rd
mode on F and the 4th mode on G are secondary scales, and their
pseudo-tonic has to be treated as a real tonic.

A thorough and intense study of the Gregorian chant is highly
rewarding, the plain chant being the greatest treasury of primary
melody, i.e. a melody in no way predetermined by chordal harmony. Its rhythm is determined solely by the text, not by a
constant musical meter. Moreover, it exemplifies syllabic as well
as melismatic treatment of the text.

Gregorian Melodies for Vocal Setting

Et e -rit in di - e il - la lux ma·gna, al - le · lu - ia.

Et e - runt pra - va in di - re - cta

et a - spe - ra in vi - as pla - nas.

Mi - se - re - re no - bis.

Tam -quam spon - sus Do - mi - nus pro -

ce - dens de tha - la - mo su - o.

Double Counterpoint at the Octave

A two-part setting which can be reversed, i.e. the two voices
exchanged by transposing the top voice an octave down or the
bottom voice an octave up, is called *double counterpoint*. Such a
setting yields two versions, both equally correct and workable.
The reversal changes the intervals between the two voices in the
following way:

$$1\ 2\ 3\ 4\ 5\ 6\ 7\ 8$$
$$8\ 7\ 6\ 5\ 4\ 3\ 2\ 1$$

Consequently, a fifth has to be treated as a fourth; it must be approached and left by step or be tied to a preceding consonance:

All other intervals retain their harmonic sense. To make possible a reversal by one octave, the distance between the two parts must not exceed an octave; otherwise one voice would have to be transposed two octaves up or down, or the lower voice one octave up and the top voice one octave down.

Imitation

Imitation is the reproduction of a melody or a melodic motive by a succeeding voice.

Orlandus Lassus: Cantiones sine Textu II

Chorale: Wachet auf ruft uns die Stimme (M. Praetorius)

Wake from   sleep!   Wake from sleep!

Wake from sleep!   Wake from

hark,   sounds   are   fal - - - -

sleep!   hark, sounds are

ling!   hark, sounds   are   fal - - -

fal - ling!   hark,

- - - - ling!

sounds   are   fal -

A. Corelli: Sonata No. 7, for Violin and Continuo

J. S. Bach: Two-Part Invention No. 4

J. S. Bach: Two-Part Invention No. 1

G. F. Handel: Sonata for Oboe and Continuo

W. A. Mozart: String Quartet in D major, K. 575

Tonal Imitation

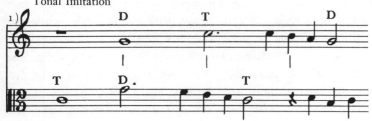

This reproduction can be at the unison with the preceding voice, or at any other interval. It can be *strict*, i.e. preserving exactly the note-values and intervals of the leading voice, or *free*, i.e. more or less approximate. It may also move in larger note-values, *augmentation*, or in smaller ones, *diminution*. It may also be inverted in *contrary motion*. Imitation carried through the whole extent of a melody, or even a whole movement, is called a *canon*. A special kind of imitation is *tonal imitation*, or the mutual correspondence of tonic and dominant. Imitation by inversion becomes strict and especially meaningful when utilizing the fact that the falling scale is the inversion of the rising scale, while the neutral scale remains the same when it is inverted.

A famous old counterpoint book gives the following recipe for the first studies in imitation, "First set a few notes at your discretion; then write them note by note in the other voice, at any interval whatsoever; after that, set against this imitating voice the appropriate notes according to the rules of counterpoint and watch for a good singable melody; that's how a two part composition comes about." The first results of this procedure, however, inevitably will be some patchwork, and only after a continued struggle through such patchwork will the student arrive at a "good singable melody." Therefore this exercise should be preceded by a search for the inherent possibilities of imitation in given melodies. Following are a few examples:

This simple little melody allows the following imitations:

By inversion

ASSIGNMENTS:

1) Search for the possible imitations in the following melodies:

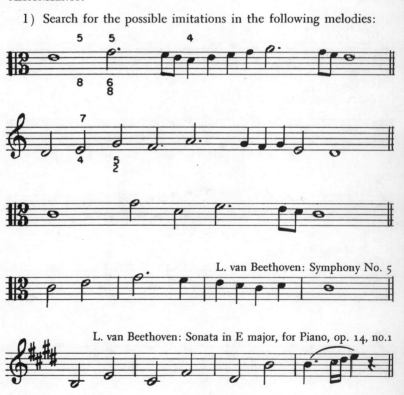

L. van Beethoven: Symphony No. 5

L. van Beethoven: Sonata in E major, for Piano, op. 14, no.1

2) Write short imitative vocal settings in the 3 basic scales and the modes of F and G. The imitation should not be carried too far; use one well-shaped motive which, after having gone through both voices, leads into a cadence.

3) Construct short two-part canons at various intervals. A rewarding exercise is to write a whole series of canons that start with the same motive, as shown in the following examples:

By contrary motion II

The ending of a canon can be fitted to its beginning so that the canon can be repeated indefinitely, as in the first and third example.

THREE-PART SETTING

The study of three-part setting consists mainly of adding a third voice to the exercises in two-part setting. The third voice has to be fitted, as a second counterpoint, into the two-part harmony established by the given melody and the first counterpoint. This, however, does not mean completing the harmony merely by filling in chords note after note; the second counterpoint should be a melody of its own, just as the first. Even a three-part setting note against note must be conceived as a texture of three melodic voices, not as a sequence of chords. The harmony instead of being materialized in chords and chord progressions, has to be imagined as an intrinsic guiding principle and moving force. Thus a polyphonic setting constitutes an intellectual harmony, while chords and chord progressions represent the sensual and material side of harmony. Both these aspects of musical harmony are indispensable, but there is no question that the first ranks higher than the second. "The invisible harmony is mightier than the visible" (Heraclitus).

Therefore in any contrapuntal work melodic considerations have to prevail. Whenever the student finds himself in a dilemma between two versions, one yielding the better melody, the other the better sounding harmony, he should decide in favor of the better melody.

Note Against Note

The third voice, added to the two-part examples note against note, is to move in the same note values as the two given parts. The exercises of this assignment should be arranged so that the given melody and both counterpoints appear in all three voices in turn, in the following order:

TOP VOICE	MIDDLE VOICE	BASS
1. Counterpoint 1	Counterpoint 2	Given Melody
2. Counterpoint 2	Given Melody	Counterpoint 1
3. Given Melody	Counterpoint 1	Counterpoint 2

Shifting the given melody to the bass or the top voice mostly will require transposition to the lower or the higher octave.

Adding a bass to a given two-part setting is more difficult than adding a middle or top voice, and the student should not be discouraged if at times a poor result seems to be more or less inevitable.

The first counterpoint should be considered unalterable, a second *given melody*. Occasionally a change of one or more notes is inevitable, especially when the lower voice, which in the original two-part example closed with a bass cadence, now becomes a middle voice, and the second counterpoint assumes the function of a bass.

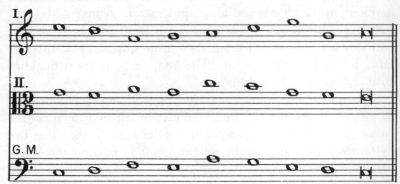

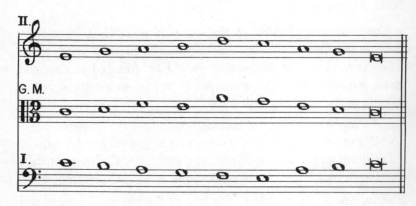

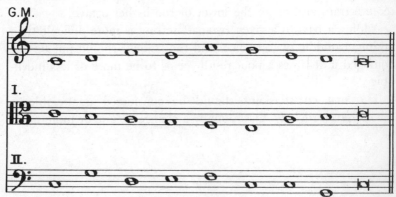

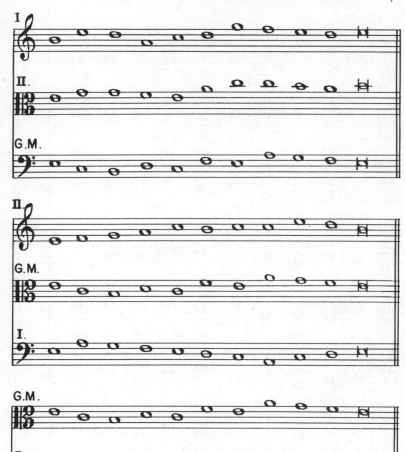

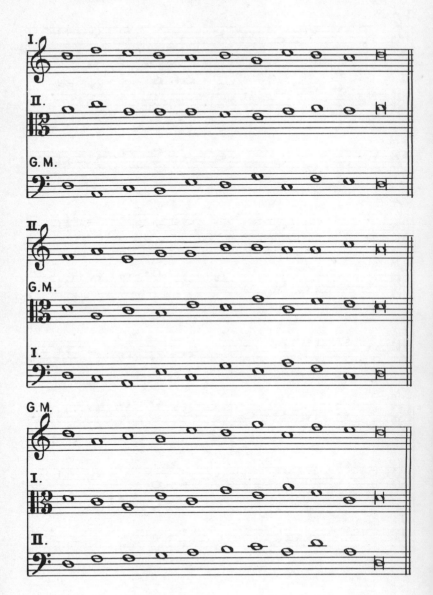

Second and Third Species Combined

To the two-part examples of two notes against one, a third voice, moving in four notes against one, is to be added, and vice versa. The three voices, *given melody, first counterpoint, second counterpoint*, should be arranged in the same three combinations as in the previous assignment.

Simultaneous dissonances in the first and second counterpoint are unobjectionable when they occur on a light beat and are conditioned by consistent and balanced voice leading as well as by a satisfactory spatial relation of the three voices. Moreover, the relation of each voice to the given melody has to be correct, according to the rules of the second and third species.

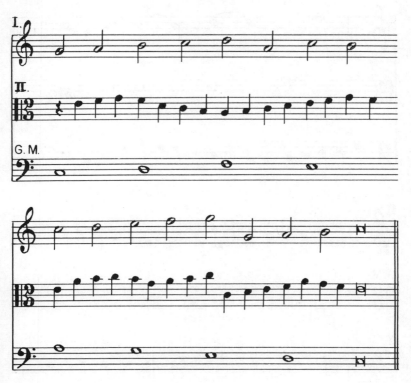

Syncopated Counterpoint

Adding a third part to the syncopated two-part examples requires some special considerations on completing the harmony, in order to put into action the full moving force of the dissonance.

Insofar as it is compatible with smooth melodic voice leading, the third tone accompanying a suspension should be chosen so that a complete triad results at the resolution. Thus the suspension of a fourth above the given melody should be accompanied by a fifth or sixth above the melody. The latter, however, is harmonically weak and should be used only for the sake of better voice leading, especially to avoid parallel fifths in a chain of fourths and thirds (see ex. b).

An upper seventh should be accompanied by a third, or by a lower fifth. In a chain of sevenths and sixths in the latter case, the fifth must alternate with the third in order to avoid parallel fifths (ex. e). A ninth must be accompanied by a third or fifth (ex. f, g).

In the bass, the suspension of a second should be accompanied by its upper fourth (ex. h), or fifth (ex. i); that of a fourth by its upper second or ninth (ex. h).

The suspension of a lower seventh, which should be used only for compelling melodic reasons, should be accompanied by its

second (ninth) or fourth when resolved downward (ex. k), and
by a fourth when resolved upward (ex. l).

Afterbeating fifths are unobjectionable. In three-part setting they become almost imperceptible, as the dissonance of the second, and consequently its resolution to the third, prevails on the fourth and its resolution to the fifth (see ex. h, above).

ASSIGNMENTS:

For the practice of syncopated counterpoint two assignments are given here, the first consisting of adding a third part in the note-values of the given melody. Here, as always, in the case of a dilemma between harmonic and melodic considerations, the latter have to prevail. The second assignment—four notes in the second counterpoint against each note of the given melody—is much more rewarding; here the third part has sufficient freedom of motion to satisfy melodic as well as harmonic requirements.

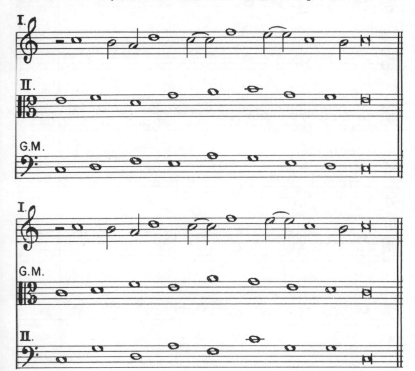

Mixed Note-Values

To the two-part settings with mixed note-values, a third voice, also moving in mixed note-values, is to be added. A well-balanced and transparent interplay of the two counterpoints will be produced best by the use of complementary rhythm. If one voice moves in shorter notes, the other stands on longer ones, and vice versa. Imitations may be used whenever they are made possible by harmony and space. Nothing needs to be added to the general rules for good three-part harmony.

Mixed Note-Values in All Three Voices—
Vocal Three-Part Settings

Once again the student has to be warned against writing too many notes. The following examples will show, better than words, how to keep a third voice rhythmically and melodically independent. Here and henceforth the following rule will prove very helpful:

When two voices move by contrary or oblique motion, a third voice may proceed in parallel thirds or sixths with one of them. When, on the contrary, the two given voices move in parallel, the third should move by contrary or oblique motion.

These exercises should be continued for a longer period.

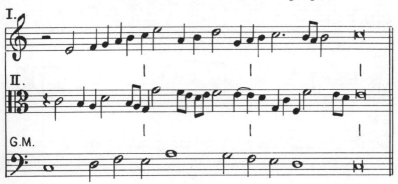

cel - - - sis De - - o.

cel - - sis De - - o.

cel - sis De - - o.

Imitation

The following exercise consists in setting two imitating voices against a given melody. Imitation, instead of being used occasionally, is to be carried through as far as possible. Strict imitation, however, is not obligatory, nor should imitation ever be forced. On the contrary it should be developed out of the possibilities afforded by the given melody and its inherent harmony, as, for instance, in the first example below; here the fundamental bass of the given melody—C G D A F C G C—invites an imitation at the upper fifth. Likewise, in the second example the given melody is accompanied by a canon in the upper fifth, very obviously born out of the inherent harmony. The third example represents a specific feature of polyphonic art, the *contrapuntal chorale arrangement*. The beginning of each line of the chorale goes, in shorter note-values, through the accompanying voices, preceding the entry of the chorale melody. This technique, invented and widely practiced by the Netherlands masters of the fifteenth and sixteenth centuries, was brought to its highest perfection by J. S. Bach in his cantatas, motets and, above all, in his chorale preludes for the organ.

There is, of course, no further obligation to work out the two counterpoints successively.

Chorale: Da Jesus an dem Kreuze stund

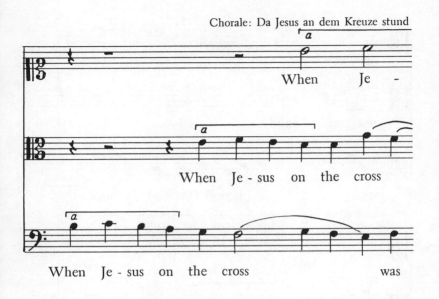

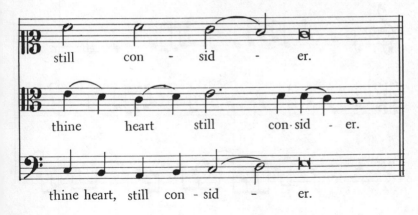

still   con - sid - er.

thine   heart   still   con· sid - er.

thine heart, still   con - sid - er.

This assignment also includes the addition of a third voice to the two-part canons of pages 66 ff.:

FOUR-PART SETTING

Homophonic Four-Part Setting

Homophony is in no way opposite to or different from poly-phony; it is merely the simplest kind of polyphony. All voices move in the same rhythm, yet each of them is an independent melody. Thus a homophonic setting, as for instance a four-part chorale, is, in general, a note-against-note setting, with occasional use of passing tones (in this case two tones are sung to one syllable). The difference between such polyphony and a "harmonized" chorale can be demonstrated easily by examining any of Bach's nearly 400 four-part chorales. Consider the first line of the chorale No. 31 from The Passion According to St. Matthew:

This four-part setting was developed by the following procedure: first, Bach set a bass-melody against the chorale-melody; next, in the space between these melodies he set two additional melodic voices, according to the harmony determined by melody and bass. In this example the tenor is very obviously the third voice, the alto the fourth. Had the two middle voices been filled in merely by completing chords, the chorale would look like this:

ASSIGNMENT:

The student should investigate at least 12 Bach chorales according to the procedure described above, first playing the two-part harmony of melody and bass, then singing through each individual voice, and finally playing the complete setting. After that, he should work out four-part settings according to Bach's procedure, which is more or less the procedure of polyphonic setting in general. Since the rise of the technique and style of thorough bass (shortly after 1600), and the subsequent development of instrumental music, the *two-part conception of melody and bass* has been the basis of composition technique.

Polyrhythmic Four-Part Setting in Double Counterpoint

A double counterpoint at the octave (in notes of various values) is to be made the basis of a four-part setting so that its two parts are made the outer voices, and two middle voices added. Then the same procedure is to be repeated with the inversion. Later, the two invertible parts should be given to the soprano and tenor, and the bass added as the second counterpoint. Here are some examples:

This most important and rewarding exercise should be applied to melodies of various kinds and continued for some time. Plain chants, chorales, folk songs, self-invented melodies are to be used. Imitation should be used wherever possible.

Chorale: Vom Himmel hoch

In the second half of this example the double counterpoint has been abandoned for the sake of the cadential steps of the bass.

Ma - gni - fi - cat   a - ni -

Ma - gni - fi - cat   a - ni -

Ma - gni - fi - cat   a - ni -

G. M.

Ma - gni - fi - cat   a - ni -

ma me - a Do - - mi - num.

ma me - a Do - - mi - num.

ma me - a Do - - mi - num.

ma me - a Do - mi - num.

G.M.

Ma - gni - fi - cat a - ni -

Ma - gni - fi - cat a - ni -

Ma - gni - fi - cat a - ni -

Ma - gni - fi - cat a - ni -

ma me - a Do - mi - num.

ma me - a Do - mi - num.

ma me - a Do - mi - num.

ma me - a Do - - mi -num.

Chorales for Exercises

Ach Gott und Herr

A - las! my God! My sins are great, My con -

science doth up - braid me; And now I

find that in my strait no man hath

pow -er to aid me.

Nun ruhen alle Wälder

Now all the woods are sleep - ing,

And night and still - ness creep - ing O'er

cit - y, man, and beast.   But

thou, my heart, a - wake thee, To

prayer a - while be - take thee, And

praise thy Mak - er ere thou rest.

Lobet den Herren

Praise Him, the High - est Om - ni -
Praise Him for - ev - er, my spir -

po - tent King of cre - a - tion!
it, thy hope of sal - va - tion!

Come   to   his   courts,   songs   and   sweet

mu — sic dis - course,   Swell - ing   in

deep   ad - o — ra   -   tion!

Ach wie flüchtig

O   how   cheat - ing,   O   how   fleet - ing   is   our

earth - ly   be   - ing!   'Tis   a   mist   in   win —

try   weath - er   Gath - ered   in   an   hour   to —

geth — er   And   as   soon   dis - persed   in   e - ther!

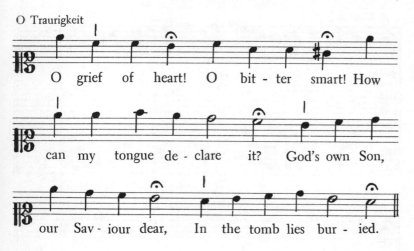

O Traurigkeit

O grief of heart! O bit - ter smart! How can my tongue de - clare it? God's own Son, our Sav - iour dear, In the tomb lies bur - ied.

Double Counterpoint at the Tenth

Inversion at the tenth changes the intervals between the two parts in the following way:

$$1 \quad 2 \quad 3 \quad 4 \quad 5 \quad 6 \quad 7 \quad 8 \quad 9 \quad 10$$
$$10 \quad 9 \quad 8 \quad 7 \quad 6 \quad 5 \quad 4 \quad 3 \quad 2 \quad 1$$

Since the third becomes an octave and the sixth becomes a fifth when inverted, it is not possible to use parallel thirds and sixths. Consequently, this double counterpoint excludes parallel motion altogether, and the two parts are mostly restricted to contrary or oblique motion. The fourth becomes the lower seventh and therefore should not be used as a suspension.

Two inversions are possible: the top voice transposed to the lower tenth and the bottom voice transposed to the upper tenth.

As one of the voices moves in parallel thirds with its transposition, both may sound simultaneously; thus any double counterpoint at the tenth yields two three-part settings. When, moreover,
the two voices also constitute a double counterpoint at the octave,
both inversions can be combined, so that a four-part setting results,
consisting of two voices, each doubled in tenths. Even more combinations are possible, by contracting the tenths into thirds or
inverting them into sixths.

Given Melody and inversion

Given Melody and inversion

Counterpoint and inversion

Counterpoint and inversion

Given Melody and inversion

Double Counterpoint at the Twelfth

Inversion at the twelfth changes the intervals as follows:

$$1 \quad 2 \quad 3 \quad 4 \quad 5 \quad 6 \quad 7 \quad 8 \quad 9 \quad 10 \quad 11 \quad 12$$
$$12 \quad 11 \quad 10 \quad 9 \quad 8 \quad 7 \quad 6 \quad 5 \quad 4 \quad 3 \quad 2 \quad 1$$

Here the upper third becomes the lower tenth, and vice versa; the sixth becomes a seventh when inverted and therefore must be treated as a dissonance.

Even more so than in the double counterpoint at the tenth, this transposition involves a change of key. As in the double counterpoint at the octave, the inverted voice cannot be used as a third voice, moving in parallel twelfths, i.e., fifths, with the counterpoint. However, turning the fifths into fourths, by inversion at the octave, yields a very usable counterpoint in parallel fourths.

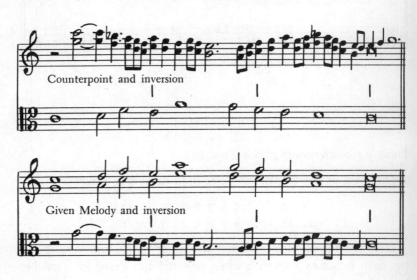

In this context the fourth has lost its ambiguity and becomes perfectly consonant. Thus the parallel fourths can be shifted to the bottom.

The double counterpoint at the twelfth, when combined with that at the tenth, allows one of the voices to be doubled in parallel thirds. Where suspensions are avoided it is even possible to double both voices, accompanying the upper voice with lower thirds, the lower voice with upper thirds.

Compared with the eminently practical value of the double counterpoint at the octave, tenth, and twelfth, the remaining possibilities of invertible counterpoint—at the seventh, the ninth, the eleventh—are of little or no importance, and are mentioned here just for the sake of a complete survey. It may be noted that in the double counterpoint at the eleventh the upper sixth becomes the lower sixth and vice versa—the only workable result of this inversion.

$$\begin{array}{cccccccccccc} 1 & 2 & 3 & 4 & 5 & 6 & 7 & 8 & 9 & 10 & 11 \\ 11 & 10 & 9 & 8 & 7 & 6 & 5 & 4 & 3 & 2 & 1 \end{array}$$

Also, the counterpoint and its inversion can be played simultaneously, with elevenths contracted into fourths.

Combinations of this kind, however, are of real artistic value only when they offer themselves within an organic musical context. Contrapuntal art should never be the mere result of calculation, and even the most artful combinations should be carried by a stream of inner life; it is this inner life that distinguishes the

genuine work of art from the mere artifice. This may be exemplified
by the following passage from Mozart's Duet in G major for
Violin and Viola.

Within four measures an inversion at the twelfth is followed by
one at the octave, and a third inversion at the eleventh. All this is
far from premeditated, it is just born out of the descending
melodic line of the viola part, thus joining the utmost simplicity
to the highest perfection of art—an example of supreme master-
ship.

APPENDIX

Studies in the Pentatonic Scale and the Double Scale

In this book for the first time the five-tone scale has been included in a comprehensive tonal system, while the double scale is here dealt with for the first time altogether. Therefore a short introduction to their contrapuntal treatment is given here.

The Pentatonic Scale

From the viewpoint of a tonal system based on the seven-tone scale, the five-tone scale appears incomplete. Yet it has to be recognized as a totality and technically treated as such, the same as any scale of seven or more tones.

It is this totality which constitutes melody as well as polyphonic harmony. This, however, means no strict limitation to the five tones of the scale. Even Chinese music, which since primordial ages has remained basically pentatonic, knows the use of a sixth and a seventh tone as passing tones. The sixth and seventh tones must be used so that they do not appear as "strange" or "wrong" tones; therefore they should be introduced by a whole step or a larger interval, not by a half step.

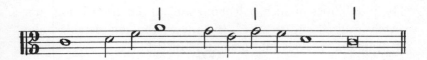

Likewise an occasional half step should not appear as a leading-tone step.

Owing to the absence of half steps and leading tones even dissonant harmonies produce little or no tension or friction. Therefore dissonant tones may proceed by leaps of thirds or sometimes even larger intervals.

There is also no strict necessity to treat fourths and sevenths as suspensions and resolve them accordingly.

Special care should be taken to assure well-proportioned spatial relations.

There is only an incomplete chordal and cadential harmony to be coördinated with the five-tone scale. Thus pentatonic polyphony has to be provided by the moving force of melody alone. The possibilities of such polyphony are still far from being completely realized and explored, in spite of the considerable influx of pentatonic melody into modern music.

The following melodies, as well as some of the student's own invention, should be used for various studies in two, three, and four parts, beginning with two-part settings in mixed note values and proceeding to three- and four-part settings. The expedient of introducing a sixth and seventh tone should be employed sparingly.

Melodies for Exercises

(Inversion of 2)

(Also the same melody inverted)

Some more extended settings are given here, exemplifying possibilities of a strict and consistent pentatonic polyphony.

American (Negro) Folk Song

Flute

Voice

I   am   a   poor   and   for - eign

stran - ger,   I   jour - ney   through   the

world   of   woe.   There   is   no   sick -

- ness,   toil   nor   dan - ger   in

that   fair   land   to   which   I   go.

I'm go - ing there   to   see   my

moth - er,   I'm   go - ing   there,   no

more   to   roam;   I'm   just   a - go -

- ing   o - ver   Jor - dan,   I'm   just   a -

go - - ing o - ver home.

Indian Folk Tune

From "Little Christmas Music," Prelude (H. K.)

The Double Scale

The double scale represents the widest range of tonality: it arranges the chromatic row of tones—which, strictly taken, is merely a musical alphabet, not a scale—in a *diatonic* order, where all tones appear as equally essential. Consequently each tone should be used according to the sense of the scale. Avoid weakening and devaluating the melody by chromatic passing tones.

The melodies given for exercises should be treated in the same way as those of the previous assignment.

In all the following examples accidentals apply only to the note immediately following.

Two Canons on the same Melody

G.M.

Melodies for Exercises

Cadences:

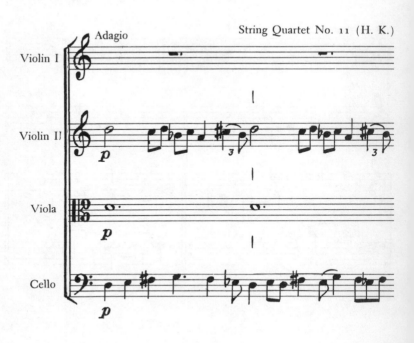

String Quartet No. 11 (H. K.)